Little Treasures

Little Treasures

A Book of Thoughts, Quotes, and Inspirations

by Sherry Chiger

SCHOLASTIC INC.
New York Toronto London Auckland Sydney
Mexico City New Delhi Hong Kong

ISBN 0-439-16116-9

Published by Scholastic Inc., 555 Broadway,
New York, NY 10012.

12 11 10 9 8 7 6 5 4 2 3 4 5/0

Printed in the U.S.A. 01
First Scholastic printing, March 2000

Contents

Little Treasures

Introduction: Say What?

You may be wondering how a book of quotations by other people can be relevant to your life. What do they, and their words, have to do with you?

Plenty, as it turns out. That's the great thing about this book: You get to see how other people, living in places and eras very different from yours, felt and thought about situations that really aren't so different from yours.

Let's suppose you're having a horrible day. You get into a fight with your brother, and your mom takes his side again, even though you're right and he's wrong. Then you have a surprise quiz in history class that you aren't ready for, and worst of all, in the lunchroom you slip and fall right into a massive ketchup spill. Not only does half of the school watch you land on your butt, but you also have to walk around the rest of the day with big red ketchup splotches on your jeans. By the time you return home, your face is as red as the stains on your pants, and you're as miserable as you've ever been. No one could possibly understand how rotten and humiliated you feel.

But then you read a quote by a poet named T. S. Eliot (1888–1965): "The only thing to do is to do nothing. Wait . . . you will find that you survive humiliation and that's an experience of incalculable value."

Hmmm, that makes sense, doesn't it? You're starting to feel a little better already.

Reading about how other people got through tough days can be reassuring: You're not the only one having a bad day, and if others can make it through, so can you!

But books of quotations aren't only filled with sayings to help you when you're down. You know how sometimes you're so happy about something or someone that you're at a loss for words? Some of the people quoted in this book were able to put together the words for you.

You can do so many things with a book like this: Choose a saying to serve as your personal motto and tape it to the inside of your locker to inspire you throughout the day. Use different quotations to personalize birthday presents, greeting cards, and thank-you notes. Read at least one quotation each night — and maybe you'll be inspired to look at your own life in a different light.

We don't know who first said all of the "little treasures" in this book; some of the sayings have been passed on for so many generations, we've lost the names of the people who said them in the first place. But the fact that their words survive, even after their names have faded away, brings us to what might be the best thing about this book: The wisdom on these pages lasts forever. No matter where your life takes you, there's bound to be a quotation here to serve you well.

Friendship Forever

Chances are you have several types of friends. There are those you sit next to in school every day, or you're friends because your parents are friends with their parents. Then there are friends you see only once a week in dance class or when you go away to camp each summer.

And then there are your special buds, your "best" friends. When they're not around, you miss them. And if you have a falling out with them, you mope and sigh and maybe even cry until you make things right with them again. You simply can't imagine your life without them.

Your best friends can be classmates, neighbors, or even members of your family. They can be boys or girls or adults. What matters is that they're always there for you, just as you are there for them. The quotations on the following pages describe just how wonderful friends can make your life. Why not share these sayings with them?

True Friends

Always have words of encouragement.

Love you unconditionally, faults and all.

Keep your secrets under lock and key.
Light up your life when you're in the dark.

Know laughter can be the best medicine.

Are never far apart even though oceans may come between them.

Weather the storm in search of the rainbow.

— Anonymous

In helping others to happiness, we are on the road to the same goal ourselves.

— Richard Cardinal Cushing (1895-1970),
American Roman Catholic Archbishop of Boston

Thoughtfulness is a gift that you can give without having to wrap it first.

— Anonymous

A friend is one who walks in when others walk out.

— Walter Winchell (1897-1972),
American journalist

It is one of the blessings of old friends that you can afford to be stupid with them.

— **Ralph Waldo Emerson (1803-1882),**
American essayist and poet

Life is a chronicle of friendship. Friends create the world anew each day. Without their loving care, courage would not suffice to keep hearts strong for life.

— **Helen Keller (1880-1968),**
American author and spokesperson for the disabled

Friendship is far more delicate than love.

— **Hester Lynch Piozzi (1741-1821),**
English writer

Friendship with oneself is all important, because without it one cannot be friends with anyone else in the world.

— Eleanor Roosevelt (1884-1962),

American author, diplomat, and humanitarian; wife of Franklin Delano Roosevelt, 32nd U.S. president

The most I can do for my friend is simply to be his friend.

— Henry David Thoreau (1817-1862),

American writer

The best thing to hold onto in this world is each other.

— Anonymous

A friend can tell you things you don't want to tell yourself.

— **Frances Ward Weller,**
contemporary American writer

Friendships are fragile things, and require as much handling as any other fragile and precious thing.

— **Randolph S. Bourne (1886-1918),**
American essayist and critic

Dreams shared with friends are dreams that survive in the light of day.

— **Anonymous**

Kind words can be short and easy to speak, but their echoes are truly endless.

— Mother Teresa (1910-1997),
Nobel laureate and humanitarian

You'll never regret sharing a smile with a friend.

— Anonymous

A smile succeeds where a thousand words might fail.

— Anonymous

A friend is a gift you give yourself.

— Robert Louis Stevenson (1850-1894),
Scottish essayist, novelist, and poet

A friend is someone who knows all about you and likes you anyway.

— Anonymous

Have patience with a friend rather than lose him forever.

— Arab proverb

True happiness consists not in a multitude of friends, but in the worth and choice of friends.

— Anonymous

One who looks for a friend without faults will find none.

— Hasidic saying

Words of friendship, comfort, and assistance need not be spoken aloud.

— Anonymous

Friends show their love in times of trouble, not in happiness.

— **Euripides (c. 484–406 B.C.),**
Greek playwright

Most of the meaningful aspects of life are closely associated with people. Even the dictionary definition of life involves people.

— **Anonymous**

A life without a friend is a life without sun.

— **German proverb**

You never have to look far to find a reason to share happiness.

— **Anonymous**

Wishing to be friends is quick work, but friendship is a slow-ripening fruit.

— **Aristotle (384–322 B.C.),** ***Greek philosopher***

When the sun shines on you, you see your friends. Friends are the thermometers by which one can judge the temperature of our fortunes.

— **Marguerite Gardiner, Countess of Blessington (1789–1849),** ***Irish writer***

A day without kindness will be gloomy no matter how much the sun shines.

— Anonymous

The act of caring is not meant to be measured.

— Anonymous

Wherever you are, it is your own friends who make your world.

— William James (1842-1910),
American psychologist and philosopher

A smile is never an ending but always a beautiful beginning.

— Anonymous

Friendship is a gift tied with an invisible golden bow.

— Anonymous

Celebrate the happiness that friends are always giving; make every day a holiday.

— Amanda Bradley,
contemporary American writer

A happy thought shared turns an ordinary day into one that shines in your memory.

— Anonymous

Everyone is beautiful when sharing laughter.

— Anonymous

No friendship can cross the path of our destiny without leaving some mark on it forever.

— François Mauriac (1885-1970),
French writer and Nobel laureate

To express yourself to a friend is to reach out and hold hands with the universe.

— **Anonymous**

A smile gently hugs the heart of the one who receives it.

— **Anonymous**

Friendship doubles our joy and divides our grief.

— **Cicero, (106-43 B.C.),** ***Roman orator, statesman, and philosopher***

To share your joy may not cost anything, but the recipient knows its value.

— Anonymous

An act of kindness is an act of caring.

— Anonymous

Friendship is the only cement that will ever hold the world together.

— Woodrow Wilson (1856-1924),
28th U.S. president

A ready smile and a warm heart will unlock the door to friendship.

— **Anonymous**

A kind word can light up the day for the giver, as well as for the recipient.

— **Anonymous**

Do not protect yourself by a fence, but rather by your friends.

— **Czech proverb**

Better to be surrounded by a circle of friends than enclosed by walls of solitude.

— Anonymous

Appreciate the gifts that each person brings to your friendship.

— Anonymous

Close friends contribute to our personal growth. They also contribute to our personal pleasure, making the music sound sweeter, the wine taste richer, the laughter ring louder because they are there.

— Judith Viorst, *contemporary American writer*

The sun always shines a little brighter when I think of you, my friend.

— **Anonymous**

You will know your true friend indeed, only when you come to her in need.

— **Anonymous**

Of all the ties that bind, friendship is the strongest.

— **Anonymous**

Friendship is love with wings.

— **Anonymous**

Best friends are like diamonds, precious and rare. False friends are like leaves, found everywhere.

— **Anonymous**

With clothes new are the best, with friends old are the best.

— **Anonymous**

You can think aloud in the presence of a friend and not regret it.

— **Anonymous**

What is a friend? A single soul dwelling in two bodies.

— **Aristotle (384-322 B.C.), Greek philosopher**

Share a happy thought with someone, and see how quickly you're given one in return.

— **Anonymous**

Am I not destroying my enemies when I make friends of them?

— Abraham Lincoln (1809-1865),
16th U.S. president

When you give the gift of friendship, it's never the wrong size.

— Anonymous

Snowflakes are one of nature's most fragile things, but just look what they do when they stick together.

— Verna Kelly, *contemporary American writer*

An act of compassion is a gift from one heart to another.

— **Anonymous**

Friendship is like a bank account; you cannot continue to draw on it without making a deposit.

— **Anonymous**

You may find friendship where you least expect it.

— **Anonymous**

A friend's worth cannot be measured.

— **Anonymous**

Like the best fruits, friendships often ripen slowly.

— **Anonymous**

There is no friend like an old friend.

— **Anonymous**

Choose friends who will bring out the best in you.

— Anonymous

Make new friends, but keep the old.
One is silver, and the other's gold.

— Anonymous

A good friend will support you in time of need, applaud you at times of success, and be there for you all the days of your life.

— Anonymous

A good friend can live far away and still be close to your heart.

— **Anonymous**

Friendships may be like the seasons, blowing hot and cold, ever changing, but always needed whatever the weather.

— **Anonymous**

Sitting in silence with a friend can speak volumes.

— **Anonymous**

So long as we are loved by others I should say that we are almost indispensable; and no man is useless while he has a friend.

— **Robert Louis Stevenson (1850–1894),**
Scottish essayist, novelist, and poet

Be wary of material gifts. The best gift a friend can bestow is her time, her concern, her self.

— **Anonymous**

The key to friendship is you. As you sow, so shall you reap.

— **Anonymous**

Who Are You?

Just as you may have different types of friends, you probably see yourself in different ways at different times. There's the happy, confident you who aces a math test or scores the winning goal in a soccer game. There's the hard-working you who spends hours practicing the piano for a recital. There's the thoughtful you who cleans up after dinner without your parents even asking.

Of course, then there's also the you who yells at your little brother or sister or is so busy playing video games that you forget to do your homework.

If lately you don't seem to remember anything but the not-so-good parts of you, these quotations might remind you of all the considerate, helpful, happy parts of your personality, your life, and yourself that you've forgotten about. You didn't lose them — sometimes you just need a few words of encouragement to rediscover them!

Think highly of yourself because the world takes you at your own estimate.

— **Anonymous**

Hope is putting faith to work when doubting would be easier.

— **Anonymous**

Self-trust is the first secret of success.

— **Ralph Waldo Emerson (1803-1882),**
American essayist and poet

Turn your stumbling blocks into stepping stones.

— **Anonymous**

Hold your head high, stick your chest out. You can make it. It gets dark sometimes, but morning comes and keeps hope alive.

— **Jesse Jackson,** ***contemporary American civil rights activist and clergyman***

Pain is never permanent.

— **Anonymous**

Sadness flies away on the wings of time.

— Anonymous

Patience is a bitter plant, but it has a sweet fruit.

— German proverb

If you are never scared or embarrassed or hurt, it means you never take any chances.

— Julia Sorel, *contemporary American writer*

Humor is the great thing, the saving thing. The minute it crops up, all our irritations and resentments slip away and a sunny spirit takes their place.

— **Mark Twain (1835-1910),** ***American writer***

Deal with the faults of others as gently as with your own.

— **Chinese proverb**

The important thing is to never stop questioning.

— **Albert Einstein (1879-1955),**
American physicist

What is begun in anger ends in shame.

—Benjamin Franklin (1706-1790), *American statesman, scientist, and philosopher*

The days that make us happy make us wise.

—John Masefield (1878-1967), *English poet laureate, playwright, and fiction writer*

Happiness doesn't depend upon who you are or what you have; it depends solely upon what you think.

—Dale Carnegie (1888-1955), *American writer and speaker*

Life is too important to take seriously.

— **Oscar Wilde (1854-1900),**
Irish poet, wit, and dramatist

Most folks are as happy as they make up their minds to be.

— **Abraham Lincoln (1809-1865),**
16th U.S. president

Make the most of yourself. That is all there is to you.

— **Ralph Waldo Emerson (1803-1882),**
American essayist and poet

How many cares one loses when one decides not to be something, but to be someone.

— Coco Chanel (1883-1971),
French fashion designer

If you do the best you can, you will find, nine times out of ten, that you have done as well as or better than anyone else.

— William Feather,
20th-century American writer

Your thoughtfulness is the perfect gift no matter what the occasion.

— Anonymous

Never be bullied into silence. Never allow yourself to be made a victim. Accept no one's definition of your life; define yourself.

— **Harvey Fierstein,** ***contemporary American playwright and actor***

This above all; to thine own self be true.

— **William Shakespeare (1564-1616),** ***English playwright and poet***

The ultimate measure of man is not where he stands in moments of comfort, but where he stands at times of challenge and controversy.

— **Martin Luther King Jr. (1929-1968),** ***American civil rights activist and clergyman***

Be content with your lot; one cannot be first in everything.

— Aesop, *legendary Greek fabulist*

Everyone thinks of changing the world, but no one thinks of changing himself.

— Leo Tolstoy (1828-1910), *Russian novelist and philosopher*

The sin isn't falling down, but staying down.

— Anonymous

Hold fast to dreams for if dreams die, life is but a broken winged bird that cannot fly.

— Langston Hughes (1902-1967),
American writer and poet

How far you go in life depends on your being tender with the young, compassionate with the aged, sympathetic with the striving, and tolerant of the weak and the strong. Because someday in life you will have been all of these.

— George Washington Carver (c. 1864-1943),
American botanist and educator

Fear less, hope more;
Whine less, breathe more;
Talk less, say more;
Hate less, love more;
And all good things are yours.

— Swedish proverb

You grow up the day you have your first real laugh at yourself.

— Ethel Barrymore (1879-1959),
American actor

When you delight in the game, the effort seems unimportant.

— Anonymous

Happiness is like jam. You can't spread even a little without getting some on yourself.

— Anonymous

Any situation can be improved with an encouraging word.

— **Anonymous**

It's the possibility of having a dream come true that makes life interesting.

— **Paulo Coelho,**
contemporary Brazilian writer

You're on the road to success when you realize that failure is only a detour.

— **Anonymous**

When we get too caught up in the busyness of the world, we lose connection with one another – and ourselves.

— **Jack Kornfield,** ***contemporary American therapist and writer***

Reach out when you feel down, and the response you receive will lift you up.

— **Anonymous**

A wise man will make more opportunities than he finds.

— **Anonymous**

Share what makes you happy and see happiness reflected on the face of everyone who looks your way.

— Anonymous

Pain is inevitable. Suffering is optional.

— Anonymous

All happiness is in the mind.

— Anonymous

He who knows enough is enough will always have enough.

— **Lao-tzu** ***(6th century B.C.), Chinese philosopher***

Always imitate the behavior of the winner when you lose.

— **Anonymous**

Our deeds determine us, as much as we determine our deeds.

— **Anonymous**

Success is a journey, not a destination.

— **Anonymous**

Happiness depends, as nature shows,
Less on exterior things than most
suppose.

— **William Cowper (1731-1800),** ***English poet***

When all think alike, no one is thinking.

— **Walter Lippmann (1889-1974),**
American journalist and author

Worry is interest paid on trouble before it falls due.

— **W. R. Inge (1860-1954),** ***English clergyman***

You must be the change you wish to see in the world.

— **Mohandas Gandhi (1869-1948),** ***Indian nationalist and spiritual leader***

To be on the cutting edge, you must need an edge to cut with. That edge is your belief in yourself, sharp and ready to go.

— **Sara Ryan,** ***contemporary American artist***

No man is an island entire of itself; every man is a part of the main.

— John Donne (1572–1631), *English poet*

If you are kind at every opportunity, you'll soon find that kindness abounds.

— Anonymous

Day after day, we discover our own lives. Because we never know what we will find. Every discovery is an unexpected gift we give ourselves.

— Barbara Esbensen,
contemporary American poet

There is much good in the worst of us,
And so much bad in the best of us,
That it hardly becomes any of us
To talk about the rest of us.

— **Anonymous**

The world belongs to the energetic.

— **Ralph Waldo Emerson (1803-1882),**
American essayist and poet

Ah, but a man's reach should
exceed his grasp,
Or what's a heaven for?

— **Robert Browning (1812-1889),**
English poet

If we had no winter, the spring
would not be so pleasant:
If we did not sometimes taste of
adversity, prosperity would
not be so welcome.

— **Anne Bradstreet (c. 1612-1672),**
American poet

The spirit is the true self.

—**Cicero (106-43 B.C.)**, ***Roman orator, statesman, and philosopher***

I had rather be right than be president.

—**Henry Clay (1777-1852)**, ***American politician***

I cannot and will not cut my conscience to fit this year's fashions.

—**Lillian Hellman (1905-1984)**, ***American playwright***

But what is Freedom? Rightly
understood,
A universal license to be good.

— **Hartley Coleridge,** ***19th-century English poet***

You are young, and your bitter recollections have time to change into sweet remembrances.

— **Alexandre Dumas,** ***19th-century French writer***

The best is yet to be.

— **Robert Browning (1812-1889),** ***English poet***

You Can Do It!

Don't you love those days when you're full of positive energy? You leap out of bed and rush to get dressed and face the day.

Unfortunately, you probably don't feel like that every day. Some mornings you might want to just pull the covers up over your head and hide. Maybe you're worried about a test, a big game, or a scary situation, like starting at a new school. Or maybe lately someone in your class has been picking on you, or your parents are stressed and are taking it out on you.

Much as you'd like to, you can't completely avoid such days and situations. But it might help you to know that everybody goes through such times — and yes, manages to get through them. You just have to remind yourself that whatever challenge or difficulty you're facing is temporary: The test won't last more than an hour, the classroom bully won't follow you the rest of your life, your parents won't be stressed and grumpy forever.

Of course, when you're especially worried or anxious, it can be tough to remember that. Luckily, the quotations on the following pages are there to remind you!

Be a "how" thinker, not an "if" thinker.

— **Anonymous**

The only limit to our realization of tomorrow will be our doubts of today.

— **Franklin Delano Roosevelt (1882–1945),** ***32nd U.S. president***

A winner is someone who recognizes his God-given talents, works his tail off to develop them into skills, and uses these skills to accomplish his goals.

— **Larry Bird,** ***contemporary American basketball player and coach***

You'll never know what's behind the door if you don't open it.

— **Anonymous**

Success is blocked by concentrating on it and planning for it. Success is shy — it won't come out while you're watching.

— **Tennessee Williams (1911-1983),**
American playwright

Always aim for achievement and forget about success.

— **Helen Hayes (1900-1993), *American actor***

Success is never final,
Failure is never fatal,
Courage always counts.

— Anonymous

There is no such word as "can't."

— Constance Clayton, *contemporary American educator*

Determine that the thing can and shall be done. And then we shall find the way.

— Abraham Lincoln (1809-1865), *16th U.S. president*

The world is before you, and you need not take it or leave it as it was when you came in.

— James Baldwin (1924-1987),
American essayist, novelist, and playwright

True life is lived when tiny changes occur.

— Leo Tolstoy (1828-1910),
Russian novelist and philosopher

Success is dependent on effort.

— Sophocles (c. 496-406 B.C.),
Greek playwright

You can't expect to hit the jackpot if you don't put a few nickels in the machine.

— Flip Wilson (1933-1999),
American entertainer

Great things are done more through courage than through wisdom.

— German proverb

If you can dream it, you can do it.

— Walt Disney (1901-1966),
American fim producer and entrepreneur

Dreams come true; without that possibility, nature would not incite us to have them.

— **John Updike,** ***contemporary American writer***

If you can't accept losing, you can't win.

— **Vince Lombardi (1913-1970),** ***American football coach***

Persistent people begin their successes where others end in failure.

— **Anonymous**

Difficulties exist to be surmounted.

— **Ralph Waldo Emerson (1803-1882),**
American essayist and poet

It takes as much courage to have tried and failed as it does to have tried and succeeded.

— **Anne Morrow Lindbergh,**
contemporary American writer

Failure is only an opportunity to begin again more intelligently.

— Henry Ford (1863-1947),
American automobile manufacturer

If there is no struggle, there is no progress.

— Frederick Douglass (1817-1895),
American abolitionist

Faith in oneself . . . is the best and safest course.

— Michelangelo (1475-1564), ***Italian sculptor, painter, architect, and poet***

Failure is impossible.

— Susan B. Anthony (1820–1906),
American reformer

When you believe you can, you can.

— Anonymous

Success is due less to ability than to zeal.

— Anonymous

Energy and persistence conquer all things.

— **Benjamin Franklin (1706–1790),** ***American statesman, scientist, and philosopher***

Worry is a slow leak that can sink the sturdiest of ships.

— **Anonymous**

Worry is a coward that disappears in the face of facts.

— **Anonymous**

Stress is an ignorant state. It believes that everything is an emergency.

— **Natalie Goldberg,**
contemporary American writer

Fears shorten our days, actions lengthen them.

— **Anonymous**

For all sad words of tongue or pen,
The saddest are these: "It might have been!"

— **John Greenleaf Whittier (1807-1892),**
American poet

Miraculous changes don't happen overnight. So take things one day at a time.

— **Anonymous**

Don't worry about failure. Worry about the chances you miss when you don't try.

— **Anonymous**

Life isn't a matter of milestones but of moments.

— **Rose Kennedy (1895-1999),** ***mother of John F. Kennedy, 35th U. S. president***

Knock the "t" off the "can't."

— **Anonymous**

Make all you can, save all you can, give all you can.

— **John Wesley (1703-1791),**
English religious leader

What the caterpillar calls the end of the world, the master calls a butterfly.

— **Richard Bach, *contemporary American writer***

Celebrities Speak Out

You may think that your favorite singers or actors have always had it easy. They were lucky enough to be born talented and good-looking, then they were discovered, and now they're rich and famous.

But because you don't read or hear about them before they were famous, you don't get to see how hard they probably had to work to get where they are. Sure, some luck may have been involved, but a fair amount of struggling was involved, too. For instance, even if you're born with a fabulous voice, you still have to practice long and hard to be able to get that voice to perform exactly as you want it to.

Because they had to work so hard and often suffered through years of self-doubt and rejection before they made it big, many celebrities have lots of wisdom to share. By reading what they have to say about their paths to success and how they gained the self-confidence to achieve their goals, you can also share their positive attitude. And by taking some of their positive energy and making it your own, you might find it easier to achieve your goals, too!

I don't want to be the next anybody. I want to be the first me!

— **Natalie Imbruglia,** ***Australian singer***

I need to please myself more than I need to please anyone else. If I can't make myself happy, there's no way I'm going to make anyone else happy.

— **Le Ann Rimes,** ***American singer***

Love bravely, live bravely, be courageous — there's really nothing to lose.

— **Jewel,** ***American singer and songwriter***

There are many complicated issues, but, hey, there are many people of good will. There are some ports in the storm.

— Bruce Springsteen, ***American singer and songwriter***

Everyone has to learn to think differently, bigger, to be open to possibilities.

— Oprah Winfrey, ***American talk show host and actor***

Treat others as you would want others to treat you. Have some fun while you're here. Don't listen to everything you hear.

— Sean "Puffy" Combs, ***American rapper and producer***

More important than talent, strength, or knowledge is the ability to laugh at yourself and enjoy the pursuit of your dreams.

— Amy Grant, *American singer and songwriter*

If you really want something, you can figure out how to make it happen.

— Cher, *American singer and actor*

A broken heart feels like the worst thing in the whole world, but it really helps you to decide what you want and don't want. You learn a lot from a broken heart.

— Jennifer Love Hewitt, ***American actor***

I have to be allowed room to do different things. . . . It's a matter of going forward and not allowing anybody to limit you.

— Julia Roberts, ***American actor***

You have to constantly try to keep in check why it is you're doing what you're doing and not let inertia carry you forward.

— Ethan Hawke, ***American actor***

This is just the real world and I'm growing up. Life is tough and it's crooked but it's pretty fantastic.

— Brad Pitt, *American actor*

If you think it's going to rain, it will.

— Clint Eastwood, *American actor and film director*

Don't take life too seriously. You've gotta take things for what they are.

— Leonardo DiCaprio, *American actor*

Whatever your dream is, whether you want to be an actress or an astronaut or a doctor or a great parent, someone will say you can't do it — and you have to know that you can.

— **Rosie O'Donnell,** ***American talk show host and actor***

It takes no more time to see the good side of life than it takes to see the bad.

— **Jimmy Buffett,** ***American singer and songwriter***

If you want the rainbow, you gotta put up with rain.

— **Dolly Parton,** ***American singer and actor***

I find comfort in different people at different times and for different reasons. I'll find comfort in a song. I'll find it in a passage in some book. I'll find it in sharing a laugh with someone.

— **James Van Der Beek,** ***contemporary American actor***

It's the moment you think you can't, that you realize you can.

— **Celine Dion,** ***Canadian singer***

I'm never going to place myself in a position where I'm doing something outside what I want to do, or what's in my heart.

— **Ice Cube,** ***American rapper and actor***

A man is a success if he gets up in the morning and goes to bed at night and in between does what he wants to do.

— Bob Dylan,
American singer and songwriter

The greatest conflicts are not between two people but between one person and himself.

— Garth Brooks,
American singer and songwriter

The joy of life is made up of obscure and seemingly mundane victories that give us our own small satisfactions.

— Billy Joel,
American singer and songwriter

I believe people should be brave, I would hate to be subject to my own cowardice.

— **Jewel,** ***American singer and songwriter***

There is no such thing as failure. Mistakes happen in your life to bring into focus more clearly who you really are.

— **Oprah Winfrey,** ***American talk show host and actor***

I truly believe that the secret to my longevity has been not giving in to the words no or can't.

— **Tyra Banks,** ***American model***

The mind is the limit. As long as the mind can envision the fact that you can do something, you can do it, as long as you really believe 100 percent.

— **Arnold Schwarzenegger,**
Austrian-American actor

Everyone needs to be valued. Everyone has the potential to give something back.

— **Diana,** ***Princess of Wales***

I'd rather be able to face myself in the bathroom mirror than be rich and famous.

— **Ani Di Franco,**
American singer and songwriter

You have to be yourself. Be very honest about who and what you are. And if people still like you, that's fine. If they don't, well, that's their problem.

— **Sting,** ***English singer and songwriter***

Just think love.

— **Lauryn Hill,** ***American singer and songwriter***

Think About It

Not all words of wisdom fit into neat categories or apply to specific situations. Some quotations are more like miniature philosophies or all-purpose mottos, but they don't have anything to do with what you're going through today or even what your life is like right now.

That doesn't mean such quotations aren't worth reading, though. Even if they don't inspire you at this moment, they may stick in your memory, and then, when you do need that sort of advice, suggestion, or insight, boom! it's waiting for you.

You can think of the quotations on the following pages as those extra few dollars you've set aside for when you might really need them, or those blankets in your closet that you don't need just yet but will be happy to have when really cold weather arrives. Sooner or later, they just might come in handy.

Don't curse the darkness; light a candle.

— Chinese proverb

When things go wrong, don't go with them.

— Anonymous

To do exactly the opposite is also a form of imitation.

— G. C. Lichtenberg, *18th-century German physicist*

He that can't endure the bad will not live to see the good.

— Yiddish proverb

Start by doing what's necessary, then what's possible, and suddenly you're doing the impossible.

— Saint Francis of Assisi (1182-1226),
Italian founder of the Franciscan orders

Imagination is more important than knowledge.

— Albert Einstein (1879-1955),
American physicist

How wonderful it is that no one need wait a single moment before starting to improve the world.

— Anne Frank (1929-1945),
German-Jewish diarist

The reward of a thing well done is to have done it.

— Ralph Waldo Emerson (1803–1882),
American essayist and poet

Hope is grief's best music.

— Anonymous

The only way to make a man trustworthy is to trust him.

— **Anonymous**

Leadership is action, not position.

— **Anonymous**

Faith is believing in things when common sense tells you not to.

— **Anonymous**

A happy thought is music to the soul.

— **Anonymous**

Thoughtfulness has a sweet language all its own.

— **Anonymous**

A smile kisses your lips with happiness.

— **Anonymous**

A smile can open doors that were securely closed.

— **Anonymous**

A smile causes the heart to dance.

— **Anonymous**

If a smile had to be bought, not even the very rich could afford one.

— **Anonymous**

Laughter does for the soul what a chocolate chip cookie does for the stomach.

— **Anonymous**

A good deed, like sunshine, will leave you warm all over.

— **Anonymous**

Life is not a race but a leisurely walk.

— **Anonymous**

The beginning is always today.

— **Mary Wollstonecraft (1759-1797),**
English writer

Life is not a matter of holding good cards, but of playing a poor hand well.

— **Robert Louis Stevenson (1850-1894),**
Scottish essayist, novelist, and poet

Life is accepting what is and working from that.

— **Gloria Gaynor,** ***contemporary American singer***

A man cannot be comfortable without his own approval.

— **Mark Twain (1835-1910),** ***American writer***

Some are born great, some achieve greatness, and some have greatness thrust upon 'em.

— **William Shakespeare (1564-1616),** ***English playwright and poet***

Genius is one percent inspiration and ninety-nine percent perspiration.

— **Thomas A. Edison (1847-1931),**
American inventor

The one who removes a mountain begins by carrying away small stones.

— **Anonymous**

Success is that old A B C — ability, breaks, and courage.

— Charles Luckman, *contemporary American architect*

Perseverance is a great element of success. If you only knock long enough and loud enough at the gate, you are sure to wake up somebody.

— Henry Wadsworth Longfellow (1807-1882), *American poet*

Look up and not down.
Look forward and not back.
Look out and not in.
Lend a hand.

— Edward Everett Hale (1822-1909),
American clergyman and author

One half of the world cannot understand the pleasures of the other.

— Jane Austen (1775-1817), ***English novelist***

What are days for?
Days are where we live
They come they wake us
Time and time over.
They are to be happy in;
Where can we live but days?

— Philip Larkin (1922-1985), ***English poet***

Each morning sees some task begin,
Each evening sees it close;
Something attempted, something
done,
Has earned a night's repose.

— Henry Wadsworth Longfellow
(1807-1882), ***American poet***

The future comes one day at a time.

— Anonymous

Imagination is the eye of the soul.

— **Joseph Joubert (1754-1824),** ***French moralist***

It is good to have an end to journey toward, but it is the journey that matters, in the end.

— **Ursula LeGuin,** ***contemporary American writer***

Kindness is the noblest weapon to conquer with.

— **American proverb**

How can we expect someone else to keep our secret if we have not been able to keep it ourselves?

— François, Duc de La Rochefoucauld (1613–1680), ***French moralist***

The greatest thing in the world is to know how to be on your own.

— Michel de Montaigne (1533–1592), ***French essayist***

Do not choose to be wrong for the sake of being different.

— Sir Herbert Louis Samuel (1870–1963),
English politician

When I hear somebody say that life is hard, I am always tempted to ask, "Compared to what?"

— Sydney J. Harris, ***20th-century American journalist***

"He means well" is useless unless he does well.

— **Plautus (c. 254–184 B.C.),** ***Roman playwright***

Daring ideas are like chessmen moved forward; they may be beaten, but they may start a winning game.

— **Johann Wolfgang von Goethe (1749–1832),**
German poet, novelist, playwright, and philosopher

Great men are they who see that the spiritual is stronger than any material force, that thoughts rule the world.

— **Ralph Waldo Emerson (1803–1882),**
American essayist and poet

Forgiveness is the key to action and freedom.

— **Hannah Arendt (1906-1975),** ***American political scientist***

If you do not think about the future, you will not have one.

— **John Galsworthy (1867-1933),** ***English novelist and playwright***

The reason that angels can fly is that they take themselves so lightly.

— **G. K. Chesterton (1874-1936),** ***English journalist and writer***

Comedy is tragedy plus time.

— **Carol Burnett,** ***contemporary American actor and entertainer***

What is now proved was once imagined.

— **William Blake (1757–1827),** ***English poet and artist***

Laughter is the shortest distance between two people.

— **Victor Borge,** ***contemporary Danish-American entertainer***

Life is what happens when you're busy making other plans.

— John Lennon (1940-1980),
English singer and songwriter

Minds are like parachutes. They only function when they are open.

— Sir James Dewar (1842-1923), ***Scottish chemist and physicist***

Imagination is the eye of the soul.

— **Joseph Joubert (1754-1824),** *French moralist*

No one can make you feel inferior without your consent.

— **Eleanor Roosevelt (1884-1962),** *American author, diplomat, and humanitarian; wife of Franklin Delano Roosevelt, 32nd U.S. president*

On the Lighter Side

Thoughts and quotes don't have to be meaningful or serious to inspire you. A very simple, funny, or even silly quote or saying can make you smile. And looking at the light, bright, humorous side of life can be the greatest inspiration of all.

A synonym is a word you use when you can't spell the word you first thought of.

— Burt Bacharach, *contemporary American composer*

If at first you don't succeed, skydiving is not for you.

— Anonymous

Don't worry about the world coming to an end today. It is already tomorrow in Australia.

— Charles Schulz, *contemporary American cartoonist*

How long a minute is depends on which side of the bathroom door you're on.

— Anonymous

Monday is a lame way to spend one-seventh of your life.

— Anonymous

Someday my ship will come in, and with my luck I'll be at the airport.

— Anonymous

The probability of someone watching you is proportional to the stupidity of your action.

— Anonymous

You can't have everything . . . where would you put it?

— Steven Wright, *contemporary American comedian*

Smile — it makes people wonder what you're thinking.

— Anonymous

When it comes to thought, some people stop at nothing.

— Anonymous

A day without sunshine is . . . night.

— Anonymous

Children are natural mimics who act like their parents despite every effort to teach them good manners.

— Anonymous

Advice is what we ask for when we already know the answer but wish we didn't.

— Erica Jong, *contemporary American writer*

'Tis better to be silent and thought a fool than to speak and remove all doubt.

— Mark Twain (1835-1910), *American writer*

Blessed is he who expects nothing, for he shall never be disappointed.

— Jonathan Swift (1667-1745), *Irish churchman and writer*

Always forgive your enemies. Nothing annoys them more.

— Oscar Wilde (1854–1900), *Irish poet, wit, and dramatist*

If stupidity got us into this mess, then why can't it get us out?

— Will Rogers (1879–1935), *American actor and humorist*

Conclusion

This book contains only a small sampling of the many words of wisdom said and written by people through the ages. If you're looking for more, you can start at the library. Many other books of quotations have been compiled. Some consist of sayings about specific topics, while others are huge encyclopedias of other people's wisdom. Biographies, poetry, and even novels often feature insightful and inspiring sayings as well.

But books aren't the only place to discover these little treasures. Pay attention to songs on the radio — after all, good songs are really poems set to music. And then there are the people around you. Believe it or not, your friends, your relatives, and your teachers sometimes utter pearls of wisdom, but because we often take those people for granted, we can easily overlook just how wise and insightful they are.

Don't overlook yourself, either. Perhaps reading the thoughts and philosophies of others has inspired you to come up with little treasures of your own! Whenever a wise thought bubbles up inside you, grab a pen and jot it down. If, days later, you think it's silly, you can always throw it away. After all, even the people quoted in this book didn't produce great sayings round-the-clock, it's just that only the truly memorable ones survived. (Perhaps they threw away the others!)

Let's suppose, though, just for a minute, that you never come up with a quotation that you feel is as good as those in this book. In the end, it doesn't really matter. Here's why, in the words of French writer Anatole France (1844-1924): "When a thing has been said and said well, have no scruple. Take it and copy it." While France's saying doesn't apply to schoolwork, it certainly applies to words of wisdom: Take them, and make them your own.